Joining Words

Conjunctions

Anita Ganeri

www.raintreepublishers.co.uk
Visit our website to find out more information about Raintree books.

To order:
☎ Phone 0845 6044371
🖨 Fax +44 (0) 1865 312263
✉ Email myorders@raintreepublishers.co.uk

Customers from outside the UK please telephone +44 1865 312262

Raintree is an imprint of Capstone Global Library Limited, a company incorporated in England and Wales having its registered office at 7 Pilgrim Street, London, EC4V 6LB – Registered company number: 6695582

Text © Capstone Global Library Limited 2012
First published in hardback in 2012
First published in paperback in 2013
The moral rights of the proprietor have been asserted.

Edited by Daniel Nunn, Rebecca Rissman, and Sian Smith
Designed by Joanna Hinton-Malivoire
Picture research by Tracy Cummins
Original illustrations © Capstone Global Library
Illustrated by Joanna Hinton-Malivoire
Production by Eirian Griffiths
Originated by Capstone Global Library Ltd
Printed in China

ISBN 978 1 406 23240 0 (hardback)
15 14 13 12 11
10 9 8 7 6 5 4 3 2 1

ISBN 978 1 406 23247 9 (paperback)
16 15 14 13 12
10 9 8 7 6 5 4 3 2 1

British Library Cataloguing in Publication Data
Ganeri, Anita, 1961-
Joining words: conjunctions. (Getting to grips with grammar)
425.7-dc22
A full catalogue record for this book is available from the British Library.

Acknowledgements
We would like to thank the following for permission to reproduce photographs and artworks: Shutterstock pp.5 (© Mark Janus), 6 (© Lane V. Erickson), 7 (© Panom), 8 (© Nattika), 10 (© Zurijeta), 11 (© Mike Flippo), 15 (© Keith Publicover), 17 (© luchschen), 20 (© ella1977), 21 (© Alena Kozlova), 23 (© Sofia), 24 (© Julien Tromeur), 26, 27 (© Monkey Business Images), 29 (© Yayayoyo).

Every effort has been made to contact copyright holders of material reproduced in this book. Any omissions will be rectified in subsequent printings if notice is given to the publisher.

Contents

Some words are shown in bold, **like this**.
You can find them in the glossary on page 31.

What is grammar?

Grammar is a set of rules that helps you to write and speak a language. Grammar is important because it helps people to understand each other.

bananas. I apples not but like,

Without grammar, this **sentence** doesn't make sense.

In grammar, words are divided into different types. These are called parts of speech. They show how words are used. This book is about the parts of speech called **conjunctions**.

I like apples, but not bananas.

Grammar turns the jumbled-up words into a sentence.

What is a conjunction?

A **conjunction** is a joining word. It helps to join words, **phrases**, **clauses**, and **sentences** together.

She plays basketball **and** tennis.

'And' is a conjunction. It joins the words 'basketball' and 'tennis'.

'And' and 'but' are both conjunctions. In the sentence below 'and' joins two words. 'But' joins a clause to a sentence.

It was warm and sunny, but I saw a cloud.

You might need to use more than one conjunction in the same sentence. They join different words, phrases, and clauses.

Spot the conjunction

Look at this list of words. Can you pick out all the **conjunctions** in the list? Remember that a conjunction is a joining word.

because

and

but

flower

swam

or

'Because', 'and', 'but', and 'or' are conjunctions. 'Flower' and 'swam' are *not* conjunctions.

Look at the two **sentences** below. How many conjunctions can you spot? There is one conjunction in the first sentence and two conjunctions in the second sentence.

The beach was narrow but sandy.

The girl had an ice cream and a lolly because she was on holiday.

In the first sentence, the conjunction is 'but'. In the second sentence, the conjunctions are 'and' and 'because'.

Joining sentences

Conjunctions are important for joining **sentences** together. Look at the two sentences below.

These two sentences don't flow very well.

Sam went swimming. Sam forgot to take his towel.

Sam went swimming, but forgot to take his towel.

You can leave out the second 'Sam' when you join the two sentences together.

You can use a conjunction to join these two sentences and make a longer sentence. It doesn't sound as awkward as the two separate sentences.

Co-ordinating conjunctions

There are different types of **conjunctions**. Each type does a different job. Here you can find out about **co-ordinating conjunctions**.

The words in this list are all co-ordinating conjunctions.

and

but

or

so

for

yet

These types of conjunctions are used to join two **sentences** together. The two sentences are just as important as each other.

An elephant is big.
A mouse is small.

These two sentences are just as important as each other.

An elephant is big and a mouse is small.

'And' is a co-ordinating conjunction. It is used to join the two sentences.

13

Subordinating conjunctions

A **subordinating conjunction** is another type of **conjunction**. It does a different job. Here you can find out about subordinating conjunctions.

because

unless

before

where

although

The words in this list are all subordinating conjunctions.

I cleaned my teeth before I went to bed.

The first part of the sentence is more important than the second part. 'Before' is a subordinating conjunction that joins the two parts of the sentence.

A subordinating conjunction joins two parts of a **sentence**. But one part of the sentence is more important than the other part.

Making contrasts

A **contrasting conjunction** is another type of **conjunction**. It does another job.

but

though

although

however

nevertheless

The words in this list are all contrasting conjunctions.

A contrasting conjunction joins two parts of a **sentence**. But the two parts say contrasting (different) things.

The pizza smelled horrible, but it tasted very nice.

The two parts of the sentence say opposite things. 'But' is a contrasting conjunction that joins the two parts.

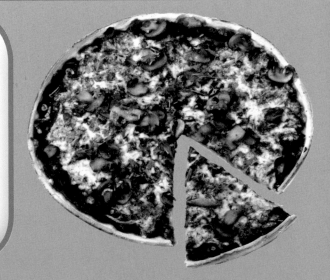

Working in pairs

Some **conjunctions** work in pairs. That means you have two words or **phrases** to add to your **sentence**.

both…and

not only…but also

either…or

neither…nor

The words in this list are all pairs of conjunctions.

In a sentence, you need to put the two conjunctions in the right places. You put them before the words you want to join.

The dinosaur is both big and strong.

'Both' and 'and' are a pair of conjunctions.

The cat not only drinks milk, but also water.

'Not only' and 'but also' are a pair of conjunctions.

19

Missing conjunctions

Practise using **conjunctions** in your own writing. They will make it flow better. Can you fill in the missing conjunction in this **sentence**?

Alice went to bed [.......] she was tired.

The missing conjunction is 'because'.

Raj didn't know [.......] to go by boat [..] car.

The missing pair of conjunctions is 'whether' and 'or'.

Look at the sentence above. Can you fill in the missing pair of conjunctions?

What is a time connective?

A **time connective** is another joining word or **phrase**. Time connectives are useful when you want to show when things happen.

The words in this list are all time connectives.

first

next

meanwhile

later

then

after a while

You can also use time connectives to show the order things happen in. Look at these three **sentences**.

'Then' and 'afterwards' are time connectives.

Mum mowed the lawn. Then I helped to pick up the grass. Afterwards, we had a glass of lemonade.

Spot the connective

Look at this list of words. Can you pick out all the **time connectives**?

finally

dragon

beautiful

after that

eventually

before

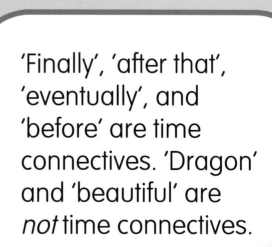

'Finally', 'after that', 'eventually', and 'before' are time connectives. 'Dragon' and 'beautiful' are *not* time connectives.

Look at the two **sentences** below. Can you spot the time connectives in each of them? There is one time connective in each sentence.

After a while, the film got boring.

Finally, the film finished.

In the first sentence, the time connective is 'after a while'. In the second sentence, the time connective is 'finally'.

Starting a sentence

You sometimes use **time connectives** at the beginning of a **sentence**.

First, the monkey peeled the banana. Then, it gobbled it up.

'First' and 'then' are time connectives at the beginning of the sentences.

26

You can use this type of time connective when you are giving instructions, for example when you are telling someone how to make a cake.

'Next' and 'finally' are time connectives that show order.

Next, mix the flour, sugar, butter, and eggs together.

Finally, put the mixture in a baking tin.

Linking sentences

You sometimes use **time connectives** to link two **sentences**. Look at the sentences below.

'Later' is a time connective that links the two sentences.

We went shopping. We went home.

We went shopping. Later, we went home.

Once there was a handsome prince. Then, he turned into a frog. After a while, a princess came by and gave him a kiss. Eventually, he turned back into a prince.

'Once', 'then', 'after a while', and 'eventually' are time connectives.

You can use time connectives like this when you are writing out a story. They help the story to flow better.

Find the joining words

Carefully read the story on this page.
How many joining words can you find?

A king lived in a far-away land. He had
a beautiful daughter, but she was always
sad. She wanted to marry a handsome
prince and live in a palace of her own,
but she couldn't find a prince. Finally,
a prince came riding by and asked the
princess to marry him. She agreed
because the prince was not only very
kind, but he was also funny.

Answers: But; and; but; finally; and; because; not only; but also

Glossary

clause a group of words that contains a verb (doing word)

conjunction joining word

contrasting conjunction conjunction that joins two sentences that each say different things

co-ordinating conjunction conjunction that joins two equally important sentences together

grammar a set of rules that helps you speak or write clearly

phrase a group of words that does not contain a verb (doing word)

sentence a group of words that makes sense on its own

subordinating conjunction conjunction that joins two sentences that are not equally important

time connective joining word or words that shows when things happen or happened

Find out more

Books

Go Further with Grammar, Ruth Thomson (Belitha Press, 2004)

Grammar and Punctuation for School (Homework Helpers), Ladybird (Ladybird Books, 2009)

Grammar Ray series, Andrew Carter (Evans Brothers, 2009)

Websites

www.bbc.co.uk/schools/ks1bitesize/literacy/conjunctions/index.shtml
Choose the correct conjunction to fill the gap and the balloon flies higher.

www.bbc.co.uk/schools/ks2bitesize/english/spelling_grammar/
Visit this BBC site to learn more about grammar and play games and quizzes.

www.primaryresources.co.uk/english/conjunctions.htm
Practise spotting conjunctions and using them to join sentences together.

Index